A SIMPLIFIED GUIDE FOR SPECIAL NEEDS AND SAFEGUARDING

BASIC GUIDE FOR TEACHING STAFF

CHRISTOPHER TYSALL

Christopher Tysall

Contents

Abbreviations

Below is a list of abbreviated terms which you will come across throughout this book and during your time in education. This list does not incorporate all the terms you will come across but covers the most frequent terms.

AAC – Augmented and Alternative Communication

ADD – Attention Deficit Disorder

ADHD – Attention Deficit Hyperactivity Disorder

ASD – Autistic Spectrum Disorder

CAMHS – Child and Adolescent Mental Health Service

CCE – Child Criminal Exploitation

CSE – Child Sexual Exploitation

DSL – Designated Safeguarding Lead

EHCP – Education and Health Care Plan

EP – Educational Psychologist

FGM – Female Genital Mutilation

HLTA – Higher Level Teaching Assistant

IEP – Individual Education Plan

KCSIE – Keeping children safe in education 2022*

LADO – Local Authority Designated Officer

LSA – Learning Support Assistant

MASH – Multi-agency Safeguarding Hub

MLD – Moderate Learning Difficulties

OCD – Obsessive Compulsive Behaviour

ODD – Oppositional Defiant Disorder

OT – Occupational Therapist

PECS – Picture Exchange Communication System

PDA – Pathological Demand Avoidance

PD – Physical Disability

PMLD – Profound and Multiple Learning Disabilities

PRU – Pupil Referral Unit

SaLT – Speech and Language Therapist

SEND – Special Educational Needs and Disability

SEMH – Social Emotional and Mental Health

SENCO – Special Educational Needs Coordinator

TA – Teaching Assistant

UNCRC – United Nations Convention on the Rights of the Child

WTTSC – Working together to safeguard children 2018*

YOI – Young Offenders Institute

"*" - Indicates year of policy used to inform this book

Introduction

This book is here to give an insight into SEND education. It will be informed mainly by the SEND Code of Practice, amongst other government and educational legislation and personal experiences. This is by no means a step by step, or how to instruction manual on SEND learners, as those who have worked with SEND learners know, there is no supplement for this. Neither is it the only set of methods or approaches available to you, as again, there are many different methods and techniques, along with many different classrooms set ups, school set ups, which can be used or applied to support our learners. This book is simply there to support you as a new teacher/LSA/TA or general classroom supporter, who is interested or has just started working with SEND learners.

Throughout the book we will look at a variety of methods to support learners. It will outline ways in which we can approach teaching SEN, how resources can be used or maximised to achieve their potential, and how the classroom can be arranged or set up to encourage and assist learners to create a suitable environment. It will look at how we support each other, through SENCO's, family support workers and external professionals such as educational psychologists, occupational therapists and speech and language therapists. We will also look at the importance of safeguarding. This, when working with SEND learners is one of the most important things, as we are the voice for many of the children we work with, especially when they are non-verbal. I have worked hard to try and recognise safeguarding concerns or issues; however, I am still learning myself. Safeguarding is not something which can sufficiently be covered in this book; however, it will be spoken about in detail to help you recognise what may be a cause for concern and what we can do to support our vulnerable young people. Finally, we will also have a look at the different areas of SEND which we may see when working in these schools. Different learning difficulties such as Autism, ADHD, global delay, and SEMH amongst others.

What is SEND?

SEND stands for Special Educational Needs or Disabilities and covers a range of needs which affects a child or young adults' ability to be educated. Their needs do not have to be physical, neither do they have to impact them physically. Needs and disabilities which can include those which affect the behaviour or ability to socialise, ability to read or write, to maintain concentration over longer periods of time, physical ability, or the ability to understand or comprehend. Some of the needs which we will look at in more detail later are SEMH, ASD, ADHD, and Global Delay.

The NHS defines SEND as a child or young person who needs special health and education support (NHS, 2022). The way in which we provide this support to access education can be achieved in a variety of ways, which will be explored as we move through this book. Children with SEND are usually support by the way of an EHCP/EHC. This is an Education, Health, and Care plan, which can be obtained through an application with the local council.

SEND is identified in different ways and by host of professionals. Parents can make self-diagnoses through the doctors, teachers in mainstream education may be able to identify early SEN needs whilst in primary/nursery schooling and there may be factors which are recognised at birth or through pre-natal screenings which may enable doctors to identify SEND. MENCAP, 2022, explains that through the identification process at an early age, specialist paediatricians may be involved to give children the best chance of accessing a suitable and inclusive education.

Areas of SEND

The SEND code of practice outlines four individual areas of SEND. The remainder of this chapter will introduce you to the different areas and using the SEND code of practice, will give some definitions of each section. The four areas are:

- Communication and Interaction
- Cognition and Learning
- Social, Emotional and Mental Health
- Sensory and/or Physical Needs

Communication and Interaction

Children with communication and interaction needs may struggle to verbalise their needs and may have difficulties understanding. Communication and Interaction also covers social rules for communication, when may be right to interject with others and what would be the right terms or tones to use at what time.

Those who may struggle most with this include children with ASD. SaLT specialists may be able to support children with aspects of communication and methods which can be used to help such as PECS, EP's may be able to provide support for those who struggle to communicate due to emotional difficulties, whilst nurture professionals may be able to support with those who may struggle to understand when may be appropriate to communicate and ways in which their communication can be appropriate for the situation.

Cognition and Learning

This section of the SEND co of practice is defined by the ability and rate at the pace in which children learn at. Children who have cognition and learning difficulties will still struggle to make progress even when work is differentiated. Children who may need support within this area have the widest range of needs including MLD, physical needs, PMLD and sensory needs. Other conditions such as dyscalculia and dyspraxia can be conditions that can affect cognition and learning. A whole host of professionals can help support within this area including OT's, EP and SaLT. Specialised resources, devices and approaches can be used to support these children; however, patience and persistence are attributes required to support these children.

Social, Emotional and Mental Health difficulties

Children and young people in this area of SEND can include children who are withdrawn from others, are rather challenging in terms of their behaviour, will disengage with education, and are often defying or disrupting others. These learners can be anxious or depressed, they can be displaying behaviour due to underlying issues in need of counselling or other support, or they can also be those who are struggling with substance abuse of self-harm. Children in this section may suffer from mental of physical difficulties. Needs for these learners may include ADHD or Autism.

Some schools may not be sufficiently equipped to support these learners, specialist teachers and TA/LSA's will be needed. There are schools that can support these learners, and these usually become named on a child's EHC to enable them the best opportunity to succeed. The SEND code of practice states that schools should have a clear procedure to help children with these needs. Many of these children will be 1:1 or 2:1 and staff may require specialist training such as team teach (a positive physical intervention method). EP's and nurture leads, along with play therapists, as well as regular counselling with specialised child therapists may be needed to assist with support for these children.

Sensory and/or Physical needs

 Children with sensory or physical needs may need some specialist provisions to support them. Their needs or disabilities may affect them from being able to access an educational curriculum. These children or young adults may be in need of short term or long-term support and the severity or need for facility may change over time. These children may have visual or hearing impairments, or may have a high sensory need, some may have a combination of more than one of these. OT's can provide specialist support for these learners, with SaLT being able to support with those who have difficulties with communication. The SEND code of practice also informs identifies children and young people with PD may require ongoing support and resources to allow them to access all opportunities available.
(SEND Code of Practice, 2015)

All four areas may cross over, and one can link to or affect the other. The specialised services can also support in more than one area, each of these will be investigated in more detail further in the book.

Resources and Methods of Support

This chapter will go over a few different methods of support. There are many others that can be used; however, the following are commonly used in primary and secondary SEND schools.

Specialised resources and support are there to be used for different reasons. Some resources allow children to access education, whilst others are there to support with areas such as communication and interaction or social or emotional needs. Resources can be physical or can be methods or approaches to support the needs of the learners.

Zones of Regulation

Many professionals use the term Zones of Regulation; however, the understanding of the term can be mixed. Leah Kuypers created the Zones of Regulation to help children to recognise when they are become less regulated and to help children manage their feelings to help them get to a healthier place. Leah created four

Zones of Regulation which are colour coded and represent different feelings.

Blue – Sadness/Boredom/Sickness
Red – Anger/Terrified/Panicked
Yellow – Worry/Frustration/Silly
Green – Happy/Calm/Proud

Each of the zones determine the feelings of the child, with the green zone being the optimal learning zone. This is where teachers will be aiming for children to be. The different zones can be difficult to recognise, for example, a child may be struggling to understand the concept of their work and be gradually heading towards the yellow zone, alternatively they may be becoming detached from their work moving slowly into the blue zone. Lessons will have been previously undertaken to help children recognise the changes in their zones and identify how they can manage them independently.

AAC

AAC is an abbreviation for augmented and alternative communication.
Augmented communication can be used to support speech, allowing a clearer understanding, this can be using Makaton or BSL, body language or gesture and the use of symbols or drawings. Whereas augmented

communication is used alongside speech, alternative communication is used when speech is difficult for the child or young person. Alternative communication can include the use of tablets or iPads, phones, or handheld communication devices. Many apps use symbols or images rather than words to help children communicate. PECS or Picture Exchange Communication System is a system which is used in many schools to support children with accessing communication. PECS can be used to make requests, to respond to mathematical questions, to identify elements of texts, and can be used alongside speech or as a sole method of communication. PECS is used in stages and helps children build their own independence.

Suitable methods and forms of AAC are usually recommended for the children by SaLT. SaLT will also provide specific training to the child and the staff enabling them to get the best from the technology ensuring everyone will have the same approach, something which is vital to AAC being successful for the child or young person.

Boxall Profiling

Boxall profiling is a tool which is used primarily with the Social, Emotional and Mental health difficulties section, as set out by the SEND code of practice. This tool is used generally by a member of the school, someone who is familiar with the children and is able to observe them in their school setting. This is often carried out by a nurture lead or a wellbeing specialist within the school. The Boxall profile is a checklist designed to work with children who may be insecure, withdrawn from their role in school, or acting out due to anger or emotional difficulties. The checklist that was designed helps teachers and support staff understand the reasons behind this behaviour, enabling them to be more supported in school and allowing more engaging educational opportunities for children. This is achieved through identification of the reasons behind the behaviour, the setting of targets for the children to work towards and tracking of the progress being made towards the target.

The test works by inputting data from the checklist into a system which gives an individual result. The result is measured against that of a competently functioning child of a representative age group. The results can then be used to help develop an IEP which ensures the child receives the best support possible.

The Boxall profile comes in two forms, one for children in primary and nursey settings, the other for children and young people in secondary schools.

NurtureUK describes the effectiveness of using the Boxall profile. It uses the Boxall childhood project to show the use the profile has on recognising SEMH in primary schools with the profile tool being able to recognise 26% of children as having moderate SEMH needs.

One of the many roles of a teacher or a TA is to support these children in line with their IEP designed with the use of the Boxall profile.

Colourful Semantics

Colourful semantics is a method which is used to support children primarily with SEND to develop sentence structure and recognising words by using symbols alongside the word with a different backing colour dependent on the use of the word. Colours associate parts of a sentence:

Who – Orange
What doing – Yellow
What – Green
Where – Blue

Much like the use of PECS, colourful semantics is implemented in stages. The initial stage starts using single words. This will be focussing on the orange colour, who. This can be done by asking questions when reading text in a small group or 1:1. Next will be combining who and what doing, and so on.

Colourful semantics is not just a resource for non-verbal learners. It can be used for those with down syndrome, ASD, language impairments or global delay.

The use of colourful semantics is not just for developing sentence structure, however, can also be used to extend sentences, respond to questions, develop the child's vocabulary and support with understanding nouns and verbs.

There are different techniques that can be used in conjunction with colourful semantics, for example, a coloured strip can be used to begin with for children to match the colours, over time the children will be able to recognise the order without using the coloured strip. Later stages include the use of different shapes and additional colours such as purple and brown and the pictures can be removed leaving just the words on the coloured cards. Finally, dependent on the ability of the learner, they could also copy the words writing them in a separate handwriting book, supporting their writing skills.

SaLT will be able to offer help and advice with the best methods and approaches to use when supporting children with colourful semantics.

Sensory resources

Sensory resources come in all shapes and sizes. Specialist rooms can be made within the school to support learners who have high sensory needs, alternatively small sensory toys can be readily available for children to have access to when they need them. Sensory resources can be used in line with some of the previous methods such as with the Zones of Regulation as a method to help calm and regulate a learner, or it could be through the Boxall profile as a way of helping a learner access education when they are feeling emotionally distracted or withdrawn.

Sensory needs can be seen in SEND and mainstream learners and can be for those who have trouble with sensory processing for a multitude of areas including touch, taste, smell, and sound.

Sensory rooms are used to support, regulate, and help initiate conversation or learning. They do not need to be expensive and can have a variety of sensory equipment to support varying levels of need. Sensory rooms are ideally a calming environment, usually using low level lighting, padded walls with soft flooring and a variety of wall textures. Lighting such as fibre optics, LED panels and light bubble tubes can provide useful calming lighting. Sensory activity can also be found in the use of water or messy play. Some sensory activities can be included in cross curricula life skill lessons such as washing clothes or dishes, or cooking using flour and dough.

As well as supporting learning, it is important to remember that sensory needs can have adverse effects in terms of accessibility to education. Learners may struggle with loud noises and or may find using water or shaving foams difficult. They may not be able to touch objects made from a particular material such as the feel of a sponge or the feel of a toothbrush. Finding ways around this may be difficult however, it is achievable and teachers and TA's of SEND learners need to be extremely creative.

A list of possible sensory resources can be inclusive of the below:

- Fidget toys
- Squishy balls
- Slime or putty
- Touch lights
- Spinning toys
- Oil lamps
- Pop toys
- Push Pull
- Coloured rice/noodles
- Sand
- Textured rollers
- Cornflour
- Flour bags/balloons

Professionals who support us

There are a variety of internal and external professionals who support the children we work with. Not including teachers and LSA/TA we will look at some of these including SENCO's, OT, EP and SaLT. This list is not restrictive and there are many more external professionals who support children in school. These are the ones you will encounter most frequently.

It is important to try and take on as much of the advice offered from these professionals, however, it is also important to offer your own insights on the learner, as you are the ones who work with them most and it is you who will be trying to implement the new methods. Everything is worth trying; however, applying the same methods will not work for every learner as they are all different and each will respond to different approaches.

What is a SENCO?

A SENCO or Special Educational Needs Coordinator is a person, or a team of people specifically designated to protect and support children with SEN. The SEND Code of Practice outlines the following key roles for a SENCO amongst others:

- To ensure all practitioners within the school/specialised setting, understand their responsibilities
- Offering support and advice for all colleagues
- Ensuring parents are supported and involved throughout the time in the setting
- Liaise with external professionals or agencies who can support SEN

(SEND Code of Practice, 2015)

The SENCO is a qualified teacher that has a specialised qualification enabling them to undertake this position. Being a qualified teacher allows them to have a different insight in the needs of the children. Part of their role is to support the class teacher in suggesting methods and strategies, resources, and interventions to support the child's progression. This type of support can be enhanced by the SENCO's involvement in the creation of the SEN policy for the school. Some of the ways this can be achieved is through observation of the child in the setting, meetings with the teachers and support assistants who work with the child, and discussions with parents. Another way the SENCO can achieve this is to apply for funding to external agencies to support both the child and the teaching staff, whether this be through interventions or staff training.

It is not uncommon to see the SENCO working amongst multiple schools, this is particularly noticed in mainstream schools, those which are slightly smaller and part of a trust or academy. Also, the SENCO does not always have a teaching responsibility, even though they are a class teacher. Along with this the SENCO will be heavily involved with the child's EHCP and will be part of the team who lead these meetings.

It is the SENCO and the school's responsibility to ensure the SENCO has the time to carry out these roles.

The SENCO has a key responsibility to ensure that all SEN learners are receiving the support and guidance that they need both in school and outside of school. They can also be a key member of the safeguarding team.

Within colleges or universities there is often a member of staff under a different title who fulfils the same or similar role.

What is SaLT

SaLT or Speech and Language Therapy has been mentioned throughout this book, but what exactly does the term mean? SaLT is there to provide a specialist assessment with regards to exactly what it stands for, speech, language, and communication. Using their specialist assessment methods, they are able to offer diagnosis, treatment options or methods and offer advice on which forms of AAC will be suitable for the students. Some of the difficulties SaLT work with are:

- Phonics
- Social communication
- Selective mutism
- Articulation
- Fluency

Assessment can be carried out using observation, 1:1 and group sessions. SaLT will often model methods for support staff and the class teacher and will regularly spend some time with the student 1:1 modelling new forms of AAC over the course of frequent 15–20-minute sessions.

SaLT will generally visit settings on a weekly basis, they will often support the setting with reports as part of the EHC and will also help provide transition materials for students moving to a new setting.

Another area in which SaLT also support is with children having eating difficulties. They offer advice on methods to use when the child is having difficulties eating, they can work with parents to create a suitable meal plan suggesting different textures and consistencies of food which will support the learner.

SaLT is usually provided through the local NHS, however, there are many private entities who can support and offer a second diagnoses.

Educational Psychologist

An Educational Psychologist or EP is a person who is trained to understand the way children develop and how they learn. Their methods use psychological approaches to produce positive outcomes in terms of access to education, communication, and child wellbeing.

Ep's work alongside schools and families to help settings support children on a mixture of difficulties. They will work either 1:1 or within a group setting, and can also work indirectly with child, on producing systems and structures within the setting, allowing them to become more inclusive towards the children they work with.

Much like the SaLT team, EP's will assess the children they work with through discussion with other professionals in the setting, observations, and interviews with the children. They will also speak with parents to help develop an understanding of how the child's home life may be affected or affecting the child in the setting. EP's will also have contact with other professionals such as doctors and social workers where needed, dependent on the individual situation of the child.

EP's will also offer support and guidance on their methods and techniques. They may do this through 1:1 training with the child's teacher or class lead, or a whole school approach in which they will provide a CPD session showing a broad range of techniques.

Just like SaLT, EPs are external agencies and can be provided either by the NHS or CAMHS, or they can be private entities which have been brought in through a contract or parent seeking an alternative approach. EP's work with children and young adults, usually up to 25 with an EHC. They will also work with a variety of needs including those suffering from SEMH or ASD.

Occupational Therapist

The SEND Code of Practice encourages schools to work closely with external providers such as educational psychologists, specialist teachers and therapists including occupational therapists or OT's.

 But what is an occupational therapist and what do they do? OT's work with individuals who have difficulties accessing their daily lives or education. They support those retuning from injury, or those who have physical, mental, or cognitive impairments. Within the school setting they may be involved in helping children to access daily functional skills such as life skills and accessing schoolwork, or to support children with their sensory or fine motor skills. Children that OT's work with include those with ASD and communication disorders. OT's use different assessments to support children and offer appropriate guidance. Much aligned with SaLT and EP, observation is the most common form of assessment. Assessments are usually observations carried out either in the classroom or playground, combined with that of gathering information from parents and carers, teaching staff and other professional reports.

Once assessment has been completed, therapy may be offered in different forms. Individual, group, and classroom sessions can be offered to help support children. They may also provide support for parents and carers, to allow them to provide some activities which can be carried out at home.

Types of therapy offered to children by OT's can be to provide support to the posture in the form of exercises and specialised seating or fine motor support using tasks such as threading, grasping objects and writing tasks. Other treatments include sensory integration which can involve swinging, push, and pull activities or bouncing and supporting concentration skills with the use of therapy putty.

Classroom setting

Classroom settings are vital to the development and access for SEN children within education. Each setting should take suitable steps to ensure education is accessible. The methods used and the classroom setup can be key. The next chapter will look over the differences and continuity that should be seen throughout a SEND child's time in education. It will also show the differences between settings and will touch on some of the different types of settings that SEND children may access.

Early Years and Primary

Some, like myself, believe that this is the most important part of a SEND learners' education. This is where they learn the fundamentals which will shape their schooling.

Communication

Assessment of communication is vital in early years. This is the where the ability or inability to communicate effectively can be best recognised. Of course, some SEND learners will develop verbal communication at a later date than that of mainstream children, however, early signs can be easily seen. SaLT will be regularly provided, and this is where stage 1 of PECS can be frequently applied. Generally, object of reference can be used within the setting to help develop early stages of communication. For example, using empty toilet rolls to resemble a request to use the toilet, or a plastic beaker to request a juice. Object of reference can also be applied to work, for example a small ruler to imply maths work or a special pencil to represent literacy lessons. Objects of reference can be placed around the classroom or placed on show at specific times in the day when needed. They can be used in conjunction with a visual timetable and should be consistent.

Messy play and sensory play

Messy play and sensory play are important for children's sensory development in the early years. Children learn about touch and smell, taste and helps develop fine motor skills. Materials that can be used to support sensory or messy play include

- Chalk
- Sand
- Play dough
- Flour
- Water

Messy/Sensory play will be carried out in a defined area, specifically for these activities. Some schools will supply an area or classroom, others will have an outside area, whilst some will define the activity my having a special floor matt that children will associate with this activity.

Structured play

At this stage there should be opportunity for structured play. It is important for SEND children at this stage to feel relaxed in a classroom, as this will define their attitudes towards classrooms for the remainder of their schooling. Structured play can be introduced in a thematic learning approach, for example, if the theme that term was the seaside, play involving beach toys or seaside play scenarios can be used. Structured play is beneficial for the children as it gives the chance for physical activity, develop social and communicational skills, and can enable children to develop confidence. These are important areas for SEND learners.

Early life skills

Here the focus should be on the basic life skills for children of this age group. For example, being able to hold a toothbrush, basic hygiene such as washing hands or using soap, or using forks or spoons to eat with. These skills can also support across the range of areas within SEND education, including developing their gross and fine motor skills, independence, and their social and communication skills.

Junior and Secondary

As children move into primary and secondary the classroom environment becomes a lot more mainstream. The toys are out of sight and used as a structured choosing activity and the sensory and messy play also become more structured and become more skills focussed.

Daily Routines

Daily routine is important in both junior and secondary school children. Routine enables structure, helps children to understand time, enables children to understand there is a start and an end, can help children develop independence for their own time management and can help ease the anxiety children have in knowing what is next.

Daily routines can be individualised and highly structured for each child early on in junior education and can become more generalised and open as they go through secondary/senior education. For example, in junior, the timetable may read as:

10-10:15 – handwriting

10:15 – 10:45 – reading

10:45 – 11:00 – break

Then as we move into senior we may see
      Lesson 1 – literacy
      Break
      Lesson 2 – Maths
We can see in senior the times have been removed and the lessons are less broken down.

Daily routines can be shown as symbols, pictures or written. In junior the use of symbols created using software such as Boardmaker or Widgit can be used. As children move towards senior education, these symbols will be replaced with pictures of the areas of curriculum, for example a picture of the sports hall for sport or pictures of maths equipment for maths, and finally towards the end of senior schooling, personalised planners or words will be used to represent lessons.

In my personal experience, symbols are used by schools for too long in a child's education. When they leave school and go to sixth form college, much of this is removed and children do not have this and struggle to adapt early on.

Academic focus

Most SEND provisions will work towards their own curriculum. This is generally made from elements of the national curriculum, adapted to support, and provide opportunities for success and achievement for learners with specific learning difficulties.

Targets are offered in line with SEND code of practice and are often set in conjunction with the child's EHCP. These can be both shorter term targets and longer term, with some to be achieved over the course of the key stage. For example, in EHCP reviews in secondary, there will be targets to be achieved by the time they reach post 16 education.

Aside from targets applied from the EHCP, schools can set an academic focus towards qualifications. Fortunately for the children we work with, there are many qualifications available, including life skills-based qualifications, key stage 2 testing and in secondary Entry Level exams for maths and literacy, or Functional skills dependent on the level.

When carrying out exams in SEND there can be a lot of support offered. Scribes, readers, transcripts can be made, braille can be offered for visually impaired, there can be additional time offered and breaks can be given. 1:1's is often provided; however, this depends on availability and the setting. In my personal experience awarding bodies are very good at offering guidelines to help provide support for SEND learners and will give advice to ensure they are able to achieve the best possible outcome.

Life skills

Life skills are generally timetabled into the curriculum in secondary and junior education. These can take place termly and are generally practical sessions. For example, cooking is often used as a life skill session and this is usually built into the thematic approach, for example, the theme could be space and the cooking life skills cooking could involve making pizza planets or fruit rocket kebabs. Life skills sessions develop as the children go through senior education. Using a washing machine, making breakfasts or dinners, hanging, and ironing clothes, even decorating an area of the school. Life skills lessons can be carried out in a classroom, however, often there are specialised rooms available for children to use. I have seen this in the form of either a life skills room or an area in the school called the flat, which has a bedroom area, living area and kitchen area, enabling children to attempt to carry out life-skill based activities.

The SEND code of practice states that from year 9 onwards the provision should be assisting the child or young person in preparation for adulthood, including independent living. Suitable life skill lessons including PSHE lessons at this point should be applied to help achieve this element of the code of practice.

Sixth Form – College

This is where we see a big shift, especially in the difference of approach and resource. In terms of the courses offered, SEND learners who attend colleges, and sixth forms are offered 1-year placements and undertake courses leading to a variety of qualifications. This is of course dependent on the sixth form. Sixth forms within a school will generally offer a placement in their school for three years, whereas sixth forms in FE establishments use yearly placements.

 The courses that can be provided generally range from life skill qualifications, which are practical, and evidence based, ideal to help prepare students for independent or supported living, up to level 1 vocational qualifications, which are ideal for the more academic learners who would be looking for work placements after education. There are also supported internship programmes, in which the college provides a work placement, for children to be placed at for the year, which would then, hopefully, lead to a full-time offer. Whilst completing the supported internship programme, students are usually completing any math or literacy qualification which they may need to support with their job.

College classrooms are a lot more clutter free, the use of a daily timetable through images of symbols are no longer visible, and signage is more course appropriate.

In terms of resources, colleges do not have the same access to funding as schools do and therefore equipment is harder to come by. When I moved from a school to an FE institute, I noticed how tough the opportunities were for resources. It is not as easy to get supplies such as colouring pens, scissors and glue sticks, or specialised equipment for writing, maths, or sports. Also access to places for outdoor learning or sport is minimal and staff from other areas of colleges are either extremely helpful or treat SEND as a distant relative, which is rather unfortunate.

PRU's

What is a PRU. PRU's are pupil referral units, and they are specialised places to provide education for those who are not able to access the same mainstream opportunities. PRU's can be for those who have behaviour difficulties, SEMH, SEND or those who have been excluded due to behaviour. They can be full time institutes or part time but should not ideally be seen as a permanent solution for children who cannot access education.

PRU's do not have to conform to the national curriculum however should be able to provide education to cover as much of the curriculum as possible. The SEND code of practice identifies PRU's as ensuring year 8 to 13 students are offered independent careers guidance. It also states that PRU's are to ensure SEN is identified and their needs are met to the best of the facilities ability, SEN children are treated inclusively with those without SEN needs and designate a responsible person to co-ordinate the SEN support within the provision.

In general, class sizes are small, with mostly 1:1 support for the children. The end goal is for children to be able to re-integrate with mainstream or an appropriate SEND provision.

Day Centres

Day centres are specialised centres which are designed to offer an alternative to education settings. They are designed to specifically meet the neds of individuals with a range of needs or disabilities, and offer different services such as lifestyle activities, educational activities, and life skills. Many of these centres are based over 52 weeks rather than term time and are much more relaxed than some of the other settings this chapter has already looked at.

 Day centres are places for young adults with SEND to have a chance to socialise, relax and develop some of their abilities which are not covered in schools or colleges. The key difference with day centres is that they are places which help enable young adults to interact with their community.

Outreach services

Outreach services can be offered in different ways. For example, schools can contact outreach services with the support and consent of the parents. In this example, they will observe the pupil within the school, identify the needs of the individual and write a support plan to meet the identified needs.

In the other example, outreach services are foundations or settings in which the children are enrolled in, and learning takes place in a variety of settings, for example, the school itself, coffees shops and sport centres or at community hubs.

The type of service offered can be determined by the individual's needs. Services seen in the second example are usually for children who have severe SEMH. They may struggle to access schools and may find it hard to be around lots of other children at once. These services offer children an alternative approach, which is specifically tailored to support them and ultimately to help with reintegrating back into educational services.

Outreach services as identified in the first example are external professionals and can provide support for learners with SEMH, SEND, ASD and their specialist outreach workers offer advice on classroom practice, teacher CPD and training, individualised curriculum, and transition amongst other areas.

Understanding diagnosis

Too many people go into education for the wrong reason. A lot of the time it is because people feel that it fits around the kids being in school, and they can get a lot of holidays, or they may also feel that it cannot be too difficult working with kids. The truth is that working with children, and especially working with SEND, is drawing, painting pictures, and playing with sand. Ultimately too many people start working with SEND children and have little to no understanding of the actual diagnosis that children have. This in turn means the child will not get their needs met and they will be missing out on achieving their fullest potential. My advice to anyone would be to undertake a level 2 or some CPD from the Open University, or other providers, based around working with children with special needs and develop some baseline knowledge before entering education.

The following descriptions of diagnosis are outlines and basic knowledge of each individual need, it is not fully comprehensive, and it is important to remember there are several approaches which can be taken when working with children with different needs. All I am offering is my personal advice and knowledge based around the needs, supported by information from academic and relevant sources.

Autism

To understand the best approaches to work with autistic children, it is important to understand the need and how it varies amongst individuals.

What is Autism? Autism is not a disease or illness; it is how the brain works and how it affects the individual. It is not something which can be cured; however, it can be managed, and medication can be provided to support individuals.

Some of the signs of autistic people can be:

- Difficulties around communication
- Struggles with loud noises
- Anxiety around changes or unknown events
- Signs of OCD
- Struggles with bright lights
- Discomfort around groups of people

Diagnosis of autism is based around two different characteristics, social communication, and interaction, and 'non-social'. Social communication and interaction highlights those who have communication difficulties or are non-verbal, and they may struggle to understand social cues such as jokes or emotions. Non-social are those who have high sensory needs and repetitive behaviours (those who enjoy doing things repetitively the same way).

Working with autistic children can be difficult and understanding the best approach may take some time. What works for one child with autism will not necessarily work with another. Some starting tips would be:

- Allow time for the child to get to know you. Trying to jump in and work with a child straight away will be difficult. Introduce yourself, whether the child is verbal or non-verbal, this is an important part of working with an autistic or any SEND child.
- Explain the day ahead but explain that there may be changes and that these are ok. With some autistic children, they will only work to a schedule and if they do not understand that there may be changes, when a change happens, they may find it difficult to respond. This is not something which may be possible from day one, and will likely take time, but new activities and changes in a child's routine can be achieved over time.
- Look for a child's reinforcer or working for reward. These can be great motivators and can help children overcome some difficulties or when learning new things.
- Consistency. Be aware of what others are doing to support the learner. If everyone works together using the same approach, the chance for success is much greater.

- Do not overwhelm the child. Too many words or too many visuals can cause a sensory overload, and this is not going to support the learner, in fact, it is likely to have the adverse effect.
- Calm tone of voice and blank expression is often helpful as this can help the child remain focussed on the task at hand, prevents the child from getting too excited and allows the child to be comfortable. Of course, a smile and a congratulations are always helpful and will help provide positive interactions, just be careful how and when they are used.

These are just some of the ways in which we can support children with autism, however, it is important to remember there are different approaches and there is not one method fits all answer.

PDA

PDA or Pathological demand avoidance is used to describe a profile of autism. PDA is a term used to describe someone who avoids everyday demands to an extreme extent (NAS, 2022). The profile of someone with PDA is:

- Resistance to everyday demands
- Uses social strategies to avoid, for example, changing the topic of conversation, leading away from the required topic

- Excessive mood swings
- Has obsessive behaviour
- Appears controlling and confident whilst being anxious

The national autistic society states that even though there has not been a lot of research carried out with regards to PDA and it is still not recognised in some countries, there are some methods which are appropriate when working with children with PDA. Allowing the learner to feel in control of the situation will be best, for example, in this approach it may be better to offer the child two different options, both which have the same desired outcome, yet they will feel in control as they are choosing the one which suits them best, giving the feeling of control.

ADHD

Attention deficit hyperactivity disorder (ADHD) is a condition which affects behaviour in children and young adults. ADHD is usually diagnosed or recognised in children between 3 and 7. ADHD can be recognised later in adolescence. The cause of ADHD is unknown; however, it is often hereditary and has been recognised as differences in how the brain functions. People with ADHD are not necessarily non-academic, in fact some of the most intelligent people to have existed have been rumoured to have ADHD, people like Albert Einstein, Thomas Edison and Alexander Graham Bell.

ADHD cannot be cured, but treatment can be offered through the use of medication or therapy. Working in schools, children will have different times when they take their medication. Some will have it before school starts, whilst other will have theirs's mid-way through the day.

Children with ADHD may struggle with many different activities including, sleeping, listening, following instructions, being organised, social situations, and getting ready for school. You may find children with ADHD may arrive late at school or may struggle to stay in the classroom. There is a form of ADHD which does not include the hyperactivity element, and this is ADD. ADHD can often be seen more in boys than in girls, however, this is mainly due to girls not showing the hyperactivity or disruptive behaviour in the same way as boys.

ADHD can show itself in conjunction with other diagnosis such as ASD, epilepsy, Tourette's, anxiety, or depression, amongst others.

Working with children with ADHD can be difficult. It is important to first remember that children with ADHD cannot help how they are behaving, they struggle to depress their impulses making it difficult for them to concentrate in a classroom. It is important to define a clear structure for the day, with specific boundaries in place. Positive instructions and lots of small tasks will help support their education. Physical activity can help children to reduce their anxiety and can improve their attention span, build in sessions like these to help enforce positive engagement in lessons.

SEMH

The SEND code of practice identifies social, emotional, and mental health difficulties as children and young people experiencing social and emotional difficulties in a variety of ways. They may present these in the form of challenging behaviour, withdrawal, or disruptive behaviour. This behaviour is usually a release for underlying mental health difficulties. They may be displayed by anxiety, self-harm, substance abuse and eating disorders.

It is the school or colleges responsibility to have clear processes in place to support these children. This type of behaviour can be extremely difficult to support which is why these processes are so important.

Working with children like this will require a lot of patience. In my experience, some people will be triggers for these children and it is important to remember this is not personal. Therefore, working with children with SEMH requires you to build a positive relationship. Find a common ground, work with the child first on their personal interests and develop upon them. Identify clear boundaries early into this relationship and as with all areas of working with children, remember to ensure they understand that you cannot keep secrets and anything they choose to tell you, you may need to report as a safeguarding concern.

 When working with SEMH, it is important to remember that something you try early on, may not work, but this does not mean it will not work later on. Revisit the method as it may take time to develop this relationship to enable the method to work.

 It is also important to remember that every day is a new day. Children with SEMH will have some great days, but also some extremely difficult ones, it is important when they return after a tough day that this day will be fresh and everything that happened the day before is in the past. Similarly, it is also important to keep your promises. If you make a promise to not just those with SEMH, but also those with SEND then you must follow through. Do not promise something you cannot deliver on.

 Finally, remember what it is like if we are having a difficult day, we would rather someone talk to us with respect and tell us the truth. Working with SEMH students, it is important for them to realise they are not the only people who make mistakes, treat them with respect, tell them you make mistakes yourself and you have difficulties, as it is just as important for their development and emotional needs, to understand adults are not perfect.

Global Delay

Global delay or global developmental delay, GDD, is a term used when it takes longer for a child to reach a particular milestone, when compared with other children of the same age. This includes fine motor skills, social interactions, or learning to walk or talk. This can be a short term, or long-term difficulty and can be an indicator of other learning difficulties.

It can be difficult to determine when to diagnose a child with global delay. This is due to children being able to carry out and develop at different rates. Therefore, it is seen as a child will be diagnosed with GDD if they are not reaching two of their man development targets by the suggested age.

Many of the previously mentioned external professionals SaLT, OT and EP may be called to support children with GDD. For support staff and teachers working with children with GDD, support can be quite varied. For example, a child may be verbal and academic, however have difficulties requiring physical therapy, in turn requiring OT support for fine or gross motor skills.

Working with GDD children it will be important to understand their individual needs and there is no generalised approach.

Positive Interventions

Something which is known; however, no one is really ever ready for is the physical behaviours that can occur as a side effect from children within SEND. These are often referred to as students with challenging behaviour. My first time witnessing this was in a behaviour class, with ASD and autistic learners who found it difficult to communicate their needs and often turned to physical attacks on staff. There are many ways this can be managed and some methods that staff will use to remove the threat of physical attacks or to intervene when the attacks are happening. Physical attacks can be peer on peer or student on staff and it can be very difficult to approach the situation in the correct manner. This chapter will have a look at some of the methods that can be used to diffuse situations. It is important to remember that in no way should a member of staff or agency, physically intervene without receiving sufficient training on how to do so.

No matter how hard we try there will be instances when challenging behaviours will occur. There could be triggers we are unaware of, triggers which are new and there can be situations that cannot be helped that can influence these behaviours such as fire alarms or a new child in the class. It is important to find the cause of what has influenced the change in behaviour and identify what can be done to solve this. Sometimes it can be quite easy, for example a distractions method, offering a time out, redirection of activity, refocus on the task or change of subject such as asking about a student's evening or weekend. These are often referred to as hands of strategies and should always be attempted before restraint.

Often children identified as having challenging behaviour have positive intervention plans or behaviour support plans in place, along with risk assessments to support the behaviours that the learner shows. Often these are in the form of a traffic light system and will usually explain the methods required to return to a green or calm state. Risk assessments and behaviour plans should be readily available for all staff and should be read and signed for by staff prior to working with that student. All behaviour plans should have gained consent from parents and should be regularly reviewed by staff and parents, for some this will be done termly, but will ideally be reviewed every six months as a minimum.

Even when we try all the methods we can think of, changing support, offering time outs, and using blank expressions and calm voices, there are times when physical interventions are required. Companies such as Team Teach, SCAPE, and MAPA amongst others, offer positive behaviour management strategies, that staff can use to intervene positively and physically should it become necessary. The methods used are a series of holds which are used to help de-escalate behaviours, until students are no longer suspected to be at risk to themselves or others. They are to be used as a last resort and should only be carried out by those who have been trained effectively to do so. It is important to be reassuring whilst using these techniques, speak with the student and continue to use diverting strategies to help support the student return to a calm state. If you have been trained to use these methods but do not feel comfortable using them, it is important to highlight that immediately, as these methods should only be carried out if you are confident in your ability to do so.

What is Safeguarding?

What is safeguarding? Safeguarding is the process in which we protect a citizen's health, wellbeing, and human rights. The NSPCC state safeguarding means protecting children and young adults from abuse and maltreatment, preventing harm to the child's development and safe and effective care, and taking all possible action to enable children and young people to have the best outcome possible (NSPCC, 2022).

The SEND code of practice advises organisations to work through the Working Together to Safeguard Children (2013, which has now been superseded by 2018) document, which is designed to offer guidance on what organisations, including individuals are required to do to safeguard and promote the welfare of children. Safeguarding law applies for children up to the age of 18, however, this does not mean that schools or colleges stop safeguarding when a child turns 18. Once a child with an EHCP turns 18 and there is a safeguarding issue, the matter will be dealt with the adult safeguarding team.

All schools and colleges will have a safeguarding policy which all staff must adhere to. Upon arrival to a new school, or prior to arrival, they will ask for you to read through at least section 1 of the Keeping children safe in education 2022 (as of September 2022) document from the department for education. Then they will ask you to read through their safeguarding policy. This policy is designed to work in line with the government requirements and guidelines to promote safeguarding and wellbeing of all students in the school or college.

All schools must have a process in place for raising a safeguard. This will usually involve the following steps:

- Raising a concern on a safeguarding form or through an electronic software introduced by the school.
- This will then be reviewed by the designated safeguarding lead, DSL, who will in line with guidance, make a decision on the next step in the process.
- The DSL will then follow the correct course, which could be talking to the parent, monitor the concern further or refer the safeguard to the MASH team (Multi- Agency Safeguarding Hub).
- At this point, depending on the previous step either the concern will continue to be monitored, if there is no further action a note will be registered on the safeguarding file, alternatively MASH will follow their process to support the child or young person.

What is considered a concern and how do we know if this is a safeguarding issue? The truth is until we follow the process we do not really know. A concern could be a student arriving in the same t-shirt or with greasy hair, this could suggest the child does not have sufficient access to basic hygiene. It could be a mark on a child's arm or leg or could be a child who has not had a hair cut in a while. Especially with non-verbal children, it is important to try and recognise something which is not a regular occurrence for a child. For example, a child may come to school daily with the same set of clothes, this may be that they only like a particular colour, not necessarily that they are wearing the same clothing, and the parents may have brought 4 sets of exactly the same clothing, however, unless this is raised initially, we will never know. My advice to anyone working with children in relation to safeguarding is to raise anything you consider as a concern. As always it is better to be safe than sorry.

KCSIE

The Keeping Children Safe in Education 2022, KCSIE, is a statutory guidance for schools and colleges. Although this does not come into force until September 2022, I felt it was worthwhile referring from this document, rather than the 2021 document. This chapter will focus on Part one of the guidance as this is what all schools and colleges will expect to be read by staff.

This guidance was issued under the Education Act, amongst others and outlines the duties that schools, and colleges must adhere to when safeguarding and promoting the welfare of children in the settings. The document is for children and young people, in which they class as those under 18.

The guidance was written to help schools and college staff understand the responsibilities of safeguarding and as mentioned previously, all staff should read at least part one of KCSIE.

What is part one?

Part one, outlines basic information schools and college staff should know. It states that it is everyone's responsibility to safeguard children. They define **everyone** as anyone who encounters children and their families. This means that you should be looking at the best interests for the child.

It also highlights, that it is everyone's responsibility to take appropriate action to identify concerns of the children. The role of safeguarding is defined in KCSIE as protecting from maltreatment, preventing the impairment of children's mental or physical health, enabling children to have the best outcome and to ensure they grow up within a safe and caring environment.

Part one of KCSIE sets out the role of school and college staff when safeguarding. This section tell staff they should be creating a safe environment for children and emphasises the importance schools have on identifying those children who may benefit from help at any point from early years to teenage years. It also references where the process that staff should follow to raise any concerns can be found later in the document. There is also the responsibility that the school must appoint a designated safeguarding lead, someone who can support staff and work with the external agencies, but also someone who is well adverse with the whole safeguarding picture and someone who is able to appropriately respond to safeguarding issues.

This document goes on to explain the roles and responsibilities in safeguarding children in schools and colleges. It tells us that staff should:

- Receive appropriate training upon induction
- Receive regular updates annually or when required
- Be aware of the process involved in making a referral for children in line with the Children Act, 1989
- Know what to do when a child tells you they are being abused, exploited, or neglected.
- Understanding how to follow the processes confidentially
- How to speak and make the child feel comfortable and approach the situation in the correct way.

What should staff look out for and what safeguarding issues are there?

Part one continues to provide guidance on key safeguarding opportunities and issues which can be identified from safeguarding. It highlights that staff should be particularly observant of children who have, mental health needs, EHCP, frequent absconder, history with alcohol or drugs, looked after child and those who are regularly absent from school, just to name a few.

KCSIE tells us that staff should be aware of indicators surrounding abuse and neglect. These indicators are categorised as Abuse, Physical abuse, Emotional abuse,

Sexual abuse, and Neglect. Due to the nature of these sections, I felt it was best to give each of these their own chapter and this will be identified further later in this handbook.

There are various safeguarding issues which staff should be able to recognise to reduce the risk of harm to a pupil. Behaviours which can be indicators of safeguarding issues can include those such as drug taking, violence, absconding and radicalisation. Safeguarding issues which KCSIE identify as those which staff should be aware of are:

- Child-on-child abuse – this can include bullying, sexual abuse including sexual harassment, physical abuse, and online abuse.
- Child Sexual/Criminal Exploitation (CSE or CCE) – some examples of CSE can be sexual abuse including kissing, touching, or watching sexual images or activities. CCE can involve forcing children into criminal activity, examples of this are working in cannabis factories, carrying weapons and shoplifting. – *KCSIE highlights the need for staff to understand that girls are at risk of CCE however indicators may be slightly different.*
- Domestic abuse – Domestic abuse can be physical, sexual, or emotional, but also psychological and financial.

- Mental Health – Staff should understand that if there are signs of a possible mental health concern of a pupil, a specialised external professional can be contacted through raising a safeguarding issue with the DSL.
- Serious violence – Indicators that a child is a victim of serious violence or is partaking in serious violence can be an increase absence from school, signs of harm, change of peer group or removal from peer group, and possible unexplainable injuries.
- Female Genital Mutilation (FGM) – Staff must follow legal guidance if there is a suspicion of FGM taking place, police should be called immediately if there is a possibility that FGM has taken place.

It is important to remember there are other safeguarding issues and these are the main ones highlighted in the KCSIE 2022.

Reporting procedures

Reporting procedures are generally identical in most settings. KCSIE 2022, identifies staff should be taking an 'it could happen here' approach, always being ready for the possible and always act in the best interests of the child. KCSIE advice states that staff should follow the organisations safeguarding procedure, highlighting the importance that the DSL should always be available for safeguarding, staff should take the action of reporting themselves rather than hoping a colleague will report the concern and a reminder that GDPR and DPA do not prevent sharing information of the child for the purpose of protecting their safety and welfare.

KCSIE advises all record keeping must be written, outlining all decisions and reasons for each decision along the way. It should be clear, comprehensive, followed up, and resolved.

This is vital as poor record keeping, failure to act and a lack of sharing information can prevent cases of abuse or neglect to be successful and can place the child back into immediate risk.

Concerns about safeguarding processes and staff

As with child safeguarding policies, schools and colleges should have policy in place to deal with staff safeguarding issues. KCSIE advises these should be identified to the principal or headteacher, and in the instances when the concern is about the headteacher or principal, these should be communicated to the governors or independent committee. Alternatively, these concerns can be raised with the LADO.

As with concerns regarding staff, if a member feels a policy is unacceptable, this can be raised using the school whistleblowing policy where this will be raised with SLT or the independent channel.

This has been a brief highlight of Part one of the KCSIE, 2022, which will come into effect in September 2022. It is worth noting that the KCSIE holds a lot more information over its five parts and offers greater information on individual sections of part one. I would advise any professional, new, or existing, to maintain their knowledge of this document, regardless of experience or level.

WTTSC

The Working Together to Safeguard Children, 2018 guidance was created through the belief that children have a right to be protected and deserve effective support as and when it is needed. The guidance ensures that all those who encounter children understands their part and how they can support children through safeguarding.

WTTSC covers three areas, it offers legislative requirements which services must follow, offers a framework for the local authority, a clinical commissioning group of a local area, and the chief officer for police of a local area to follow allowing them to identify and respond to safeguarding needs. Thirdly, it provides a framework for children death reviews.

This guidance applies to all schools, including independent, non-maintained and nurseries, it applies to all children up to the age of 18 regardless of their living arrangements, and should be read by all practitioners and organisations.

The WTTSC guidance takes a child centred approach to safeguarding. It states that all safeguarding should be approached with the child at the centre of the decision making, how would our next step affect the child? So how can this be achieved? The guidance tells us to enable this to happen we need to speak to the children and listen. Take their concerns seriously and trat them with respect. Work collaboratively when supporting children and ensure to take specific approaches to support all children regardless of their background, ability, or language. The child centred approach works in line with other documentation such as the Children Act 1989, the Equality Act 2010, and the UNCRC, the latter of which is there to recognise the rights of the child, including the rights to expression and receiving information. Using this document practitioners can support children effectively and have a child centred approach.

Responsibility

This document makes it clear that the responsibility for safeguarding is everyone's and whilst maintaining a child centred approach, to enable this to happen a co-ordinated approach is required by everyone. WTTSC states that everyone has a responsibility to keep children safe, and it is not one person's sole responsibility. To achieve this, practitioners need to work collaboratively with children, families, agencies, and organisations. Whilst working together, understanding the individual role each must play is also important. The guidance here offers key roles for individuals advising how these can be promoted by the local authority, including mayors and the police and crime commissioner.

How is this document structured?

This guidance is separated into five chapters each discussing a different area of supporting children through safeguarding. These are Assessment, Organisational responsibilities, Multi-Agency safeguarding arrangements, improving child protection, and safeguarding practice, and Child death reviews. The remainder of this chapter will discuss some of the key points from these chapters. I can only advise to download this document from the gov website for a more in depth understanding of the document.

Assessment

This chapter looks at the different elements of assessment and how early assessment can support children. It then goes on to discuss the importance of assessment for different types of children.

Early help is extremely effective at providing support for the welfare of the children we work with. It can prevent possible safeguarding incidents from progressing any further, provide the right type of care and support network from an early point. WTTSC highlights the following groups of children who may benefit from early help:

- Disabled/SEND (regardless of EHCP status)
- Young carer

- At risk of involvement with; Drugs, Alcohol, trafficking, radicalisation or exploitation and slavery
- Frequent absconder
- Looked after child or recently returned from care

Of course, this list is not exclusive, and all children would benefit from early help, this list highlights those at higher risk.

Is it important to understand the purpose of assessment when discussing safeguarding. It is not necessarily to see what is wrong, it is more to try and understand how we can help. As practitioners we have a duty to support children when there may be safeguarding concerns. WTTSC tells us assessment should be used to analyse the needs and understand what risks and how detrimental they may be to the child, whether these are likely to cause serious or significant harm and in turn, provide opportunities to address the needs and support the child keeping them safe and protected from any further difficulties. The guidance also outlines the focus on outcomes that can be achieved through effective early assessment.

This part of the guidance also offers a section discussing myths around safeguarding. Below are the main points discussed:

- There is no data protection barrier when safeguarding and consent is not needed to share information
- Personal information *can* be shared between organisations or agencies in order to protect the needs and welfare of the child
- There are no Human Rights being broken when sharing the information regarding safeguarding
- IT systems are allowed to be used when sharing information, especially when discussing supporting and safeguarding children

This section of guidance continues to offer appropriate flow charts to help support how the decision-making process regarding strategies and frameworks to support children. It uses legislation including the Children Act 1989 to inform the charts. To see these please read pages 35 through 57 of this guidance.

Organisational responsibilities

This chapter starts in line with Section 11 of the Children Act 2004, which is key in defining the duties organisations, individuals, and agencies have to ensure their organisation promote the safeguarding and welfare of children. It then goes on to highlight the roles different services have on safeguarding children.

When discussing organisations and agencies, Section 11 of the Children Act 2004 identifies the following as having statutory duties when promoting the protection and welfare of children, these are:

- Local authorities and district councils that provide children services, including sport, leisure and children and adult social care, amongst others
- Police and transport police
- Young offenders' institutes and youth offending teams
- Directors of Secure training centres and Principles of secure colleges
- NHS Trusts and other NHS organisations

To support in line with section 11, it is advised these organisations have a clear line of accountability, have a specific or designated person in charge of promoting child safety and welfare, effective recruitment strategy and staff who are able to promote, exhibit and have competent safeguarding abilities.

To be successful as an organisation it is important to be able to regularly review this information. For schools, colleges, and educational providers, WTTSC states they have a duty to safeguard and promote the welfare of children, highlighting that the guidance in its entirety relates to all schools and must work in line with KCSIE. Looking further into the guidance's recommendations for early years and childcare settings, it states that they must have understanding of issues children in their care may come across, have strict policy and procedure along with up-to-date training and knowledge of safeguarding, as well as having a designated person who has completed child protection training.

The remainder of this chapter goes on to look at the variety of different services and the duties they should adhere to when safeguarding and promoting the welfare of a child. As this book is primarily for teaching staff, I will not go over these, however, if these are of interest to you, they can be found on pages 62 to 74.

Multi-Agency safeguarding arrangements

This chapter is designed to highlight the safeguarding responsibilities that agencies have to support children and young people.

The cooperation of the multiple agencies that work with children is important for successful safeguarding. Chapter 3 of the guidance highlights the importance of these agencies joining with the three safeguarding partners to safeguard children in the local area. The three safeguarding partners are defined in the guidance in line with the Children Act 2004 as

1.   The local authority

2.	The clinical commissioning group for the area
3.	The chief police officer for the local authority area

It states that these safeguarding partners should set out a clear set of instructions including roles and duties for agencies and organisations within the local authority whilst coordinating a suitable strategy to support child welfare and safeguarding. To ensure they are effective, the strategy should be clear and cohesive, identifying areas for training and to promote effective methods for sharing information and identifying early assessment opportunity.

What are the expectations for schools, colleges, and educational providers? WTTSC tells us that these providers are pivotal in safeguarding and promoting positive welfare for children. The safeguarding partners are required to meet and become fully engaged in the safeguarding measures. The partners will look to name these facilities as relevant agencies, once named the facility has a duty to cooperate in line with the published arrangements from the safeguarding partners.

Publication of arrangements should include who the three local safeguarding partners are, the agencies they will work with and why they have been chosen, how safeguarding partners will use information and how the arrangements will be child centred, amongst others.

Improving child protection and safeguarding practice

This chapter is here to explain the importance of reviewing the services involved in child safeguarding. It then goes on to explain the processes involved under the review and how these are carried out locally and nationally. Review is important in every aspect of education. We review if a lesson has gone well or not, and the reasons it may not have been successful if this is the case. With safeguarding this is even more important as improving the measures set out can be vital to saving a child's life. This chapter highlights the use of the Child Safeguarding Practice Review Panel (the Panel) as being responsible for looking at safeguarding incidents at a national and local level. This Panel is responsible for reviewing cases, the effectiveness of safeguarding capability, whether a review is needed, what improvements need to be made and what they may identify as areas of concern. It is important to note, this Panel will investigate serious child safeguarding incidents, these include the abuse or neglect of a child and as a result the child has been seriously harmed or has died. Serious harm is defined in the WTTSC as a child who has serious and/or longer-term impairment to their social, emotional, or behavioural development, physical and mental health, it is not exclusive to the above.

The process

Once a local authority knows of a possible serious safeguarding incident, it must, in line with the Children Act 2004, notify the Panel as well as the Safeguarding Partners. Along with the Panel the Secretary of State and Ofsted if a child has died. Once the serious incident reaches the safeguarding partners, they must decide whether there needs to be a **local** review or not. For this to happen, particular criteria must be considered. These are:

- Does the case highlight improvements needed, including when improvements have been previously instated?
- Does the case highlight and reoccurring themes?
- Does the case concern two or more agencies working together?
- Has the Panel considered a local review may be necessary?

It is important to recognise that there can be instances where a serious harmful incident has not occurred, rather there has been a possible incident narrowly averted and therefore as a way of good practice a review is carried out.

This guidance advises safeguarding partners will carry out a rapid review. This is used to support the partners in what steps should be taken next, potential opportunities to respond to the incident and avoid a reoccurrence, what immediate action, if any, is required and gather facts about the incident.

When commissioning a local review, safeguarding partners need to consider reviewers. This is an important part of the process, and they should only consider professionals who has professional knowledge and understanding of safeguarding practice, strong understanding of safeguarding issues, someone who is able to understand the viewpoint rather than the hindsight and someone who has no conflicts of interest. Once decided the method of review needs to be agreed.

The report should identify a summary of recommended improvements and an analysis outlining the reasons why actions were or were not taken. It should be used as a tool to understand why and identify how an event of serious harm has happened, reducing the risk of it happening again.

The Panel also need to determine if a national review needs to be carried out. Using the case information including the feedback from the rapid review the Panel need to answer their own criteria:

- Does the case require improvements needed to promote safeguarding, including if there have already been improvements made?

- Does the case raise legislation changes to guidance?
- Does the case highlight recurrent themes?

The Panel may also take into account other evidence including doctors' reports, police reports school reports amongst others.

Once a decision is made, the Panel must notify the Secretary of state, communicating with safeguarding partners on their required involvement and discuss their rationale behind the decision with families.

In the same way the safeguarding partners select a reviewer for their local review, the Panel must also choose a reviewer who can undertake the national review. There are the same requirements for the national reviewer as the local reviewer.

The expectations for the Panel's review are however slightly different. The final report should identify improvements to promote the safeguarding and welfare of children and should also highlight reasons why actions were not taken. Unless it is deemed inappropriate, the report must be published and be public for three years as a minimum. Reports should be completed within six months and can be used by the national government to improve safeguarding systems.

Child death reviews

Finally, this chapter outlines the responsibilities of child death reviews and the responsibilities that other organisations and agencies have within child death reviews.

Child death reviews are for children under the age of 18 regardless their cause of death. This section states that all local organisations that was involved in cases, should co-operate to support the review. The review process if a child dies is as follows:

- Child Death Overview Panel (CDOP) is used to notify the child death review partners
- Practitioners should respond to understand the cause of death, the factors of death, any support the family requires and to ensure statutory obligations are met.
- A Joint Agency Response may then be required if there were external causes, a sudden unexpected death, whilst in care, unnatural causes or still birth (where there was no healthcare professional in presence).

Depending on the outcomes, if abuse or neglect was suggested as a possible cause of death, the Child

Safeguarding Practice Review Panel must be informed immediately.

Along with understanding the cause of death the child death review process is there to provide ongoing support to all involved in the incidents leading to the death – including family and organisations, a way of improving safeguarding and promoting the welfare of the child along with being there to support any criminal investigations which may be required.

Documents Summary

The differences between the two guidance can be seen and highlights just how many people are involved in the safeguarding process from you, a practitioner recognising a possible safeguarding concern, to where it may end up, with the Panel outlining recommendations for government legislation. KCSIE is primarily based at those who work in education, whilst WTTSC is a broader document, covering the roles different organisations have, whilst outlining processes for escalation of concerns from organisation level through to government officials. The key is that if our role of practitioners is completed effectively, safeguarding and welfare is promoted efficiently then there should be no serious harm incidents for children.

The areas of abuse and neglect

What is considered as abuse? We should not discuss safeguarding without identifying the terms for abuse and neglect. Keeping Children Safe in Education 2022, define abuse as a form of maltreatment of a child. Abuse falls into four different categories, Physical abuse, Emotional abuse, Sexual abuse, and neglect. Below are some explanations of each element.

Working together to safeguard children, 2018, highlight their definition of abuse in point 12 where they define abuse and neglect as sexual, physical, and emotional abuse, neglect, plus the following:

- Domestic abuse
- Controlling or coercive behaviour
- Exploitation by gangs and criminal groups
- Trafficking
- Online abuse
- Sexual exploitation
- Influences towards radicalisation

The NSPCC, 2022, identifies abuse as having long lasting impacts on children's lives and recognise different elements of abuse. Those which have not already been mentioned by the WTTSC, 2018, and KCSIE, 2022 are FGM, bullying or peer on peer abuse and protection from county lines (terminology inclusive of several forms of abuse including exploitation, gangs, and grooming).

Although there are many areas of abuse to consider the next four chapters will cover the key areas outlines in KCSIE, 2022, physical, emotional, sexual and neglect. Some of the following may become difficult to read. It is only my intention here to highlight what is outlined in the documentation. Please feel free at any point to take a moment away to gather your thoughts. Writing this was just as difficult.

Physical abuse

Working together to safeguard children and Keeping children safe in education both identify physical abuse as a form of abuse which may involve hitting, shaking, throwing, or causing any physical harm to a child. This can be caused by a parent or carer who fabricates or induces illness in a child.

Signs such as bruising, or cuts do not always suggest physical abuse is taking part. Kids as we know can be quite clumsy and can often be quite boisterous and therefor trips and falls are highly likely in younger children. Signs to look out for in this case are when a child has regular injuries, often in the same part of the body or can be similar injuries, for example a frequent bruising in the same location, or bruising appearing at significant times, for example, when a child stays with another parent at weekends or when a family member visits.

Physical abuse symptoms can include bruises, broken bones, burns or bite marks. It is important to note that bite marks may be self-inflicted, however, self-inflicted bite marks can be signs of a child managing their emotions when being exposed to physical abuse. Effects of abuse on a child can be shown as anxiety, eating disorders, depression, suicidal tendencies, and struggles with alcohol and drugs.

Emotional abuse

Emotional abuse is defined in both WTTSC and KCSIE as a persistent emotional maltreatment of a child, causing them adverse effects on their emotional development. This may cause the child to feel inadequate, anxious, unvalued, and worthless. This type of abuse may include opportunities someone has to mock or belittle either by commenting on the way a child dresses or speaks, what views they hold or how they look. Emotional abuse can also be present when hearing or seeing others being abused or neglected. This type of abuse may be an outcome of physical abuse including cyber bullying and is often seen in other areas of abuse and neglect.

Signs of emotional abuse are difficult to notice, as children can use different coping mechanisms to manage their emotions. In some instances, there may be a change in diet or a lack of or increased intake of food. Children may distance themselves from friendship groups or act immaturely to gain attention. They may overcompensate and be considerably outspoken or can become recluse and remove themselves from any conversation. Relationships with friendship groups may also begin to deteriorate or relationships with unsavoury characters may be developed. It is important to look for any changes in behaviour and report these as early as possible. As mentioned prior to this, early help can be key with safeguarding and protecting the welfare of children and young people.

Noticing the signs in early years children can be extremely difficult and these can show themselves in different ways. Things to look out for can include not having a strong bond with their parent or showing strong signs of affection for adults not within their family group. A lack of confidence or signs of anxiety are also indicators as are signs of aggression to other children or animals.

Any child can be at risk of emotional abuse, from any age and those suffering emotional abuse are often at risk of other forms of abuse. Emotional abuse is not necessarily directed at a child either. It may be a side effect from family difficulties, for example families going through a bereavement or money problems. It can also be from arguments between parents or seeing alcohol or substance abuse around the home.

Emotional abuse can impact different areas of a child's development. For instance, it can lead to difficulties conveying emotion themselves or being unable to show emotions, causing problems with relationships in later life. There can also be mental health difficulties which can lead to self-harm, including depression or suicidal thoughts, or alcohol and drug abuse. It can also lead to behavioural difficulties which could lead to stealing or bullying along with a risk or being involved in gangs or terrorist groups.

Sexual abuse

It is understandable that this chapter may cause some emotional distress. Please understand that this chapter is vital to safeguarding and outlines key signs and definitions of sexual abuse which helps support us in the safeguarding and welfare of children and young people. Please take moments away from this chapter if you find anything distressing, but please remember as practitioners we need to have a full understanding of all types of abuse.

The KCSIE and WTTSC document describes sexual abuse as that which involves forcing or enticing any form of sexual activity. This does not have to be violent and can involve both physical sexual abuse in terms of both penetrative, sex or rape, and non-penetrative sexual acts such as kissing or touching children outside of clothing. Sexual abuse can also include non-physical abuse such as looking at sexual images or grooming a child. Sexual abuse can take place online or in-person and the abusers are not always males, they can also be female and there can also be peer on peer abuse. Sexual abuse does not have to include acts of violence and it can take place online with technology being used as a tool to facilitate sexual abuse.

Signs can be quite difficult to recognise. It could be through becoming withdrawn or distant, to a child who seems to be communicating with new people. They could become increasingly secretive of who they are talking to or could be seen wearing more clothes than usual to hide physical signs of sexual abuse. Physical signs can include cuts and bruising, pregnancy, sexually transmitted infections, soreness around their private areas or other marks including bites and restraints. Signs similar with other forms of abuse include self-harm, alcohol, or drug abuse, eating disorders or changes in their emotions.

Sexual abuse is something which can happen anywhere. There is contact and non-contact abuse. Contact is physical and includes sexually touching any part of a child's body, with or without clothing, using any item or body part to penetrate a child and forcing a child to undress, touch or take part in any sexual activity.

Non-contact can include any form of sexual abuse where a child is not touched by an abuser. This can be both in person and online. Types of sexual abuse which are classed as non-contact can be forcing the child to watch pornography or view images of a sexual nature, the abuser flashing or exposing themselves and taking part in any grooming or child sexual exploitation.

Child sexual exploitation CSE and grooming are two common forms of sexual abuse. CSE is described in KCSIE as something which can occur over time or as a one off. It can involve the sharing of sexual images or videos of a child without their knowledge. CSE includes pictures or videos being shared of a child even if they are 16 or 17 and can legally have sex. Children who are exposed to CSE by a stranger or someone they consider to be in a faithful romantic relationship with.

Children can be groomed into this type of sexual abuse. Groomers build a relationship with a victim. They can be any race, age, or gender, and can groom a child over a long or short period of time. They can groom children online or in-person and this can take on a variety of guises. Some of these are:

- The use of online chat rooms
- Any online game which has a chat room (either through verbal means or written)
- Group chats or messaging services such as Discord, WhatsApp, and Twitter amongst others

Ways that grooming can be achieved are through pretending that they are younger than they are, pretending to be friends, buying gifts, or providing children with alcohol and gaining trust with the victim.

Signs of being groomed are very much the same as those that cover sexual abuse. Drinking or alcohol abuse, being secretive about who they are talking to, withdrawing themselves from their peer groups, absconding or eating disorders.

Just as with groomers, children being groomed can be either boys or girls and generally children will know the person who they are being groomed by. Children with disabilities and learning difficulties may be more at risk, as they may be unable to understand the differences between a person who is supporting them and one who is grooming them.

Neglect

KCSIE and WTTSC describe neglect as the failure to meet the basic needs for a child, including failing to provide food, clothing, and shelter, placing the child in emotional harm or danger, inadequate offering for basic medical care and can also include a lack of response to the emotional needs of a child.

Radford 2011, cited by the NSPCC, 2022 tells us that 1 in 10 children have suffered neglect. Neglect can be classified in four different areas:

- Physical neglect – this constitutes as neglecting the basic needs of a child including food, clothing, or shelter
- Educational neglect – schools or early years education
- Emotional neglect – this is neglecting the basic emotional needs of a child and can be evident in those who ignore children, isolate, or humiliate them
- Medical neglect – this is preventing the child from having sufficient healthcare such as that of access to a doctor or a dentist

Signs a child may be experiencing any of the above can be difficult to recognise. It can be seen in their bodily hygiene and appearance, for example wearing clothing on a continuous basis or lack of access to basic hygiene.

Health issues, which can be seen when children are consistently ill, shows a loss of body weight or lacking their age- appropriate vaccinations. Also, mentioning that they may be left alone a lot of the time or in their room by themselves for much of the night can indicate neglect within the household.

Neglect can hold many lasting effects on a child or young person. They can struggle to reach minimum developmental goals and can have a high chance of developing medical issues. They may consistently abscond from the family home and can also fail to have long lasting relationships. Children at risk may be those in care or with learning difficulties, along with looked after children and those with a disability.

Neglect may be deliberate; however, it can also arise from difficulties that parents or carers may be having themselves. Safeguarding can help provide support to the child, but this support can be in a way of supporting the child's provider. They may not intentionally be neglecting the child and may need support themselves. This can be seen frequently, unfortunately, with parents and carers of families with many children, or those who have children with SEND. These parents or carers may be struggling to provide the support needed to their child and unable to ask for support themselves. They may also be unaware of the support that can be provided to them or unfamiliar of the methods or external support they can use to best support their child.

It is important to remember that neglect can be unintentional and as mentioned before, support at an early stage can provide the best outcome for the child.

What to do if someone reveals abuse or neglect

There are many different things you can do as a practitioner to support a child who reveals a safeguarding issue. Before anything is considered it is important to remember the schools or organisation policy when following any specific procedure.

For us to be able to work with a child it is vital to be able to get as much information from the child as possible. Any piece of vital evidence or information missing can lead to delays in the safeguarding process and can lead to further implications for the child.

For a child to be able to talk to you about the type of abuse or neglect they are going through, there are some things suggested by the NSPCC which are useful to support the child. Listen to their claim, ensure they understand that you will not keep any secrets from anyone and that whatever they tell you will be taken seriously. It is also important for the child to realise that it is not their fault and that they are doing the right thing by speaking with someone. It is also important for the child to have an understanding of what will happen once they have given their account. This will also help them feel a lot more relaxed, as understanding the outcome can help the child feel less anxious about the unknown.

Other ways a child can be supported whilst revealing a safeguarding incident is to offer them something to drink to help them feel relaxed, give them breaks should they need them and allow for them to have a favoured member of staff available to provide some emotional support.

MASH

Multi Agency Safeguarding Hubs have been introduced to support the effective use of sharing information between agencies supporting the safeguarding and welfare of children. They were introduced due to the consequences highlighted by high profile cases such as the heart-breaking case of Daniel Pelka, where information was not shared effectively across agencies.

The government review in July 2014, Multi Agency Working and Information Sharing Project Final Report, (Carried out in 2013), highlighted the significant impact these MASH's can have on protecting children and young people. A review of 37 local authorities found that over half of the local authorities introduced Multi Agency models (referred to as MASH) to help support three areas of need when developing good practice in safeguarding, these are information sharing, joint decision making and coordinated interventions.

So, what of the impact of MASH? The government review tells us independent research carried out by the University of Greenwich found that MASH had resulted in 5% more cases being escalated as serious and a 7% reduction in cases being de- escalated. Likewise in Staffordshire and Stoke-on- Trent, 27% of cases were escalated from single agencies through the use of MASH.

The impact here is undeniable, and although these cases may not have resulted in serious harm, (which is unknown) that's over a quarter of all cases which may not have even been escalated at all if not for their intervention. Along with the impact on escalation, it was also noted that there was a better understanding between professionals and a greater use of process and resource. Other benefits that were identified was the ability to rotate staff, provide additional training opportunities and offer joint training opportunities.

What are the barriers for MASH? The report identified several main barriers including:

- Misunderstanding of what information can be shared
- Some had concerns regarding sharing information
- Risk of not being able to support adults due to the focus on children
- Struggle understanding different cultures
- Lack of performance review

A concerning barrier that was mentioned was the lack of clarity for who is accountable for a situation. This is where communication becomes key as understanding the chain of responsibility

can be vital to supporting the safeguarding and welfare needs of a child or young adult.

Services involved within the MASH differ on local authority, however, most services seem to include, the police, health services, housing teams, social workers, victim support and CAHMS. These services can be used when a referral is sent from an organisation. Once received, the agencies within MASH will share the information and decide where the support is needed. An advantage of using the MASH is the speed in which a referral can be supported, which should ensure the safety of a child.

LADO

The LADO or Local Authority Designated Officer is an individual who is appointed by the Local Authorities. They are the designated person for dealing with any allegation made which relates to a professional or person who is working with children and that is alleged to have, in line with WTTSC, 2018, either behaved intentionally to harm or cause harm against a child, carried out a criminal offense against or related to a child, posed any risk toward a child causing risk or dangers towards the welfare of a child, or someone who may be unsuitable to work with children. The report of these possible offences must be communicated to LADO as soon as possible no later than one working day. In turn they will consider three options from the allegations. Those are, is it a possible criminal offence, should the employer consider disciplinary action towards the alleged offender and is the child in need of external agency support.

Professionals who allegations could be made against may include the police, teachers, support workers, early years professionals, youth club employees, among others as well as employers such as schools, YOI or other child services.

So, what does the LADO do? The LADO is there to oversee and direct investigations ensuring all investigations are carried out thoroughly and fairly. Part of the role of the LADO is to ensure the outcomes are relayed to those involved, however will not have direct communication with those who have made the allegations. LADO are responsible for providing a proactive response, offering advice and support, managing communications with external or internal agencies, and ensuring the case is dealt with in a proficient and timely manner. They are also responsible for ensuring the case is managed without prejudices or biases and referring the case to the correct channels, should it be required, for example, the police or social care services (NLN, 2020).

If the LADO decides there is to be no further action, they should record the decision and reasons behind the verdict for further information, and relay suitable information to the persons involved.

There are instances where the LADO cannot reach a decision. In these circumstances they will reach out to an independent person who will undertake an independent review

With regards to schools and the guidance offered by the KCSIE 2022, the LADO is the chosen person should you as a member of the teaching staff have a safeguarding concern about a headteacher or principle who may be causing any risk as outlined in the WTTCS mentioned previously.

It is important when making an allegation to the LADO that you have as much information as possible. For example, mentioning what happened, times and dates, witnesses and CCTV opportunities, names of individuals involved, and contact details.

When an investigation is being carried out schools should not be suspending staff immediately. Where possible, in line with KCSIE, schools and colleges should only suspend as a last resort or only considered where there is a risk of harm. Schools will consult with the LADO regarding the member of staff continuing their role whilst under investigation. Where suspension is the only option, this will be discussed with the LADO and notification must be made with the individual within one day outlining reasons behind the suspension. Similar rules are also in place for agency staff. The LADO and school will discuss the agency member of staff and schools should not cease using an agency member without first having these discussions.

There are of course situations where there are malicious or unfounded allegations made against an individual or individuals. In these circumstances when no further action is deemed necessary, it is part of the LADO's role to provide support and guidance to enable them to return to work without prejudice or discrimination, or to feel unfairly victimised by others. The LADO will also deem whether it is necessary or not for the accuser to receive additional help and support, as this may be a cry for intervention or may be a sign of a further safeguarding issue.

The role of a LADO therefore is quite a broad and challenging one. They are there to provide support and guidance as well as offer responses and oversee reviews of challenging situations, as well as needing to be able to recognise safeguarding issues. They need to be able to communicate their findings to organisations and agencies and must be able to do this in an efficient and timely manner. A wrong decision or outcome could have extremely worrying outcomes for children and young people.

Safeguarding is something which can be spoken about at a much greater length than this, and this is a basic introduction to some of the key elements. I would recommend reading the Keeping Children Safe in Education 2021 and Working Together to Safeguard Children 2018 documents to help support your knowledge to a greater extent. There are also some fantastic websites available to support your understanding of safeguarding such as the NSPCC which have a whole host of information going into each area of safeguarding in more depth. Finally, you can also speak with your DSL on ways in which your organisation can help you to develop your knowledge of safeguarding practices.

About the author

My name is Christopher Tysall and I have been working in SEND education for the last 5 years. When I started working in a SEND school, I had no idea what to expect. I had done Level 2 courses and CPD, I had even started an education degree, however still felt I was walking into the unknown and wondered if I would be able to get up to speed quick enough. SEND education is very fast paced and you need to be able to hit the ground running. Understanding what to do, what to expect and the best ways to help are all things I had to learn as I was working. Fortunately, I was able to adapt quite quickly, however for many others there is an initial struggle to understand what to do. There is some material available, however it can be confusing and difficult to really understand, especially when a lot of what is readily available, is by people who have no real understanding of what it is like to actually work in SEND, and what people really can do to support you. After finishing my degree in 2022, I decided it was the right time for me to write something to help others. My aim is for this book to help give others an insight into learners with Special Educations Needs and Disabilities, how to help them and how to help yourselves to support these learners in the best possible way, an opportunity which I never had.

Contact

Along with being an author within SEND education, I also provide educational talks and support to businesses, schools and colleges who work with children and young people with Special Educational Needs and Disabilities, advising on best practice and classroom set-up, amongst other elements. To discuss how I can help please feel free to email me or reach out on social media and I will be more than happy to discuss options.

christophertysall@gmail.com

Thank you

References

Colourful Semantics, 2022. [online] Available at: https://www.lscft.nhs.uk/media/Site%20Images/CITNS/ Documents%20-%20SLT/Comm%200- 5y/Colourful%20semantics.pdf [Accessed May 2022].

Emotional abuse, NSPCC, 2022, [online], Available at: *https://www.nspcc.org.uk/what-is-child-abuse/types-of- abuse/emotional-abuse/* (Accessed July 2022)

England, N., 2022. *NHS England » Special educational needs and disability (SEND).* [online] England.nhs.uk. Available at: https://www.england.nhs.uk/learning- disabilities/care/children-young-people/send/ [Accessed July 2022].

Grooming, NSPCC, 2022, [online], Available at: *https://www.nspcc.org.uk/what-is-child-abuse/types-of- abuse/grooming/* (Accessed July 2022)

GOV.UK. 2022. *Children with special educational needs and disabilities (SEND).* [online] Available at: https://www.gov.uk/children-with-special-educational- needs [Accessed June 2022].

Keeping Children Safe in Education, 2021, [online] Available at:

https://assets.publishing.service.gov.uk/government/upl oads/system/uploads/attachment_data/file/1021914/K CSIE_2021_September_guidance.pdf [Accessed May 2022].

Keeping Children Safe in Education, 2022, [online] Available at: *https://assets.publishing.service.gov.uk/government/upl oads/system/uploads/attachment_data/file/1080047/K CSIE_2022_revised.pdf* [Accessed July 2022].

Mencap. 2022. *Global developmental delay.* [online] Available at: https://www.mencap.org.uk/learning-disability-explained/conditions/global-development-delay [Accessed May 2022].

Mencap. 2022. *SEND system.* [online] Available at: https://www.mencap.org.uk/advice-and-support/children-and-young-people/send-system [Accessed June 2022].

Morley, D. et al. (2017) 'Making reasonable adjustments for pupils with special educational needs and disabilities: pre-service teachers' perceptions of an online support resource', British journal of special education, 44(2), pp. 203–219. doi:10.1111/1467-8578.12175. (Accessed May 2022)

Multi Agency Working and Information Sharing Project Final Report, 2014, [online], Available at: *https://assets.publishing.service.gov.uk/government/upl oads/system/uploads/attachment_data/file/338875/MA SH.pdf* [Accessed July 2022]

Neglect, NSPCC, 2022, [online], Available at: https://www.nspcc.org.uk/what-is-child-abuse/types-of-abuse/neglect/ (Accessed June 2022)

New.boxallprofile.org. 2022. *Boxall*. [online] Available at: https://new.boxallprofile.org/#contact [Accessed May 2022].

NHS.uk. 2022. *What is autism?* [online] Available at: https://www.nhs.uk/conditions/autism/what-is-autism/ [Accessed July 2022].

NSPCC Learning, 2022, *Child abuse and neglect | NSPCC Learning*, [online] Available at: https://learning.nspcc.org.uk/child-abuse-and-neglect [Accessed July 2022]

NSPCC Learning. 2022. Safeguarding children and child protection | NSPCC Learning. [online] Available at: https://learning.nspcc.org.uk/safeguarding-child-protection [Accessed July 2022].

NurtureUK. 2022. The nurtureuk guide to implementing Mental Health and Behaviour in Schools - NurtureUK.

[online] Available at: https://www.nurtureuk.org/the-nurtureuk-guide-to-implementing-mental-health-and-behaviour-in-schools/ [Accessed May 2022].

Physical abuse, NSPCC, 2022, [online], Available at https://www.nspcc.org.uk/what-is-child-abuse/types-of-abuse/physical-abuse/ (Accessed July 2022)

SEND Advice Surrey. 2022. *Pupil Referral Units (PRU).* [online] Available at: https://sendadvicesurrey.org.uk/pupil-referral-units-pru/ [Accessed July 2022].

SEND Code of practice, 2015, [online], Available at https://assets.publishing.service.gov.uk/government/uploads/system/uploads/attachment_data/file/398815/SEND_Code_of_Practice_January_2015.pdf (Accessed May 2022)

Sexual abuse, NSPCC, 2022, [online], Available at https://www.nspcc.org.uk/what-is-child-abuse/types-of-abuse/child-sexual-abuse/ (Accessed June 2022)

THE ZONES OF REGULATION: A SOCIAL EMOTIONAL LEARNING PATHWAY TO REGULATION. 2022. *Schoolwide Implementation.* [online] Available at: https://www.zonesofregulation.com/schoolwide-implementation.html [Accessed June 2022].

Team Teach, 2022, [online], Available at: *https://www.teamteach.co.uk/about-us/* (Accessed July 2022)

The Role of the Local Authority Designated Officer, 2020, [online], Available at, https://national-lado-network.co.uk/the-role-of-the-lado-local-authority-designated-officer/ (Accessed June 2022)

Tips for Working with Individuals on the Autism Spectrum, 2020, [online], Available at *https://www.autism-society.org/living-with-autism/autism-through-the-lifespan/adulthood/employment/tips-working-individuals-autism-spectrum/* (Accessed July 2022)

Woodley, H., 2022. *Tips For Working with Social, Emotional and Mental Health Learners.* [online] TeacherToolkit. Available at: https://www.teachertoolkit.co.uk/2017/03/14/mental-health-2/#_ [Accessed July 2022].

Working together to safeguard children, 2018, [online], Available at *https://assets.publishing.service.gov.uk/government/uploads/system/uploads/attachment_data/file/942454/Working_together_to_safeguard_children_inter_agency_guidance.pdf* (Accessed June 2022)

www.ingramcontent.com/pod-product-compliance
Lightning Source LLC
Chambersburg PA
CBHW051436150726
48000CB00005B/2129